Narcissism

Avoid The Gas Lighting Effect And Liberate Yourself
From Emotional And Narcissistic Abuse

(How To Recover From Abusive Relationships And Emotional Mistreatment)

Marcel Rupprecht

TABLE OF CONTENT

Chapter 1: Who Is A Narcissist 1

Chapter 2: Traits Of Grandiose Narcissism 8

Chapter 3: Tipping Point 12

Chapter 4: They Never Offer An Apology Because They Believe They Are Always Right. 23

Chapter 5: They Also Hardly Ever Apologize Because They Never Believe They Are Wrong. 25

Chapter 6: Narcissistic Abuse Cycle 38

Chapter 7: What To Do In Response To Signs Of Emotional Manipulation 41

Chapter 8: Tips For Surviving The Breakup 48

Chapter 9: Adaptive Strategies To Help You Avoid 56

Chapter 10: Do Individuals With Narcissism Enjoy Kissing? 63

Chapter 11: Disordered Narcissism 65

Chapter 12: Can A Narcissistic Change? 73

Chapter 13: The Overt Narcissist 84

Chapter 1: Who Is A Narcissist

These characteristics are moderately stable over time and are not primarily attributable to a disease, medication use, or a person's developmental stage. Experts have also studied a less extreme form of selfishness known as the self-absorbed personality type. Despite exhibiting most or all of the characteristics of the egotistical behavioral disorder, these individuals are considered to be within the normal range of personality.

People who exhibit egotistical behavioral conditions or the egotistical personality type are preoccupied with maintaining unreasonable self-beliefs.

They become overly concerned with receiving positive, magnified criticism from others and react with exaggeratedly positive or negative emotions when they receive or do not receive confirmation that others respect them. Egomaniacs require positive feedback about themselves, and they exert effective control over others to demand or coerce respect from them. Similarly, it is recalled that selfishness resembles a type of persistent relational confidence guideline.

Self-report surveys, such as the Narcissistic Personality Inventory (NPI), the most widely used scale, are used to assess the egotistical personality type and can also be used to evaluate self-involved behavioral conditions. The NPI provides respondents with a series of constrained decision tasks in which they must determine which of two assertions is most representative of them. People completing the NPI would discover, for instance, whether they are best characterized by "individuals generally appear to perceive my position" or "being an authority doesn't mean that much to me." High NPI scorers have been shown to exhibit a wide variety of self-absorbed behaviors, including haughtiness, feigned predominance, and aggression. In addition, individuals with a clinical diagnosis of egotistical behavioral disorder score higher on the NPI than those with other mental diagnoses or control groups.

HEALTH CONCERNS

Concerns about your physical or mental health may be influencing you. Abuseinduced stress that persists over time may result in physical illness. A wide range of mental disorders, such as anxiety, depression, alcoholism, and drug abuse, may also be present.

WONDER WHY OTHERS TREASURE THEIR FAMILIES SO MUCH

A narcissistic family is more likely to cause you misery than to provide safety. You may find it unbelievable that other people appear to value their families so deeply and enjoy life.

Recovering From Narcissistic Parents

Now is the time to take the first step toward healing from this traumatic childhood experience.

RECOGNIZE NARCISSISM

Recognizing that you are not responsible for the emotional abuse you received as a child is a crucial step in the healing process. Regardless of how much their parents try to deceive them and imply otherwise, abused children are not to blame.

SET HEALTHY BOUNDARIES WITH NARCISSISTIC PARENTS

Adult children of narcissistic parents must develop healthy boundaries and appropriate relationships. For your mental health, it may be necessary or even desirable for you to sever the violent ties with your abusive parents. You are not required to endure awkward parent-child relationships.

CREATE A SUPPORT NETWORK

Those who have not been raised by narcissists cannot typically comprehend what it is like. Your friends may try to help, but end up saying things that hurt you more. Therefore, the easiest way to obtain social support is to seek out local support groups and individuals with similar experiences. Develop a support system that can help you develop self-supporting/coping behaviours and endure stressful situations.

WORKOUT AND MEDITATION

Meditation and exercise may improve your mood and strengthen your immune system, which has been weakened over time by excessive stress.

DO NOT TRY TO CHANGE THEM

Narcissists are incapable of seeing themselves as they truly are. They believe they are right and that anyone who disagrees with them is wrong throughout their entire lives. Attempting to alter them will cause you additional discomfort.

Chapter 2: Traits Of Grandiose Narcissism

The first characteristic of grandiose narcissists is that they exaggerate their positive qualities, especially their intelligence. They are notorious for their vanity, arrogance, superficiality, obsession with power, and, of course, their haughtiness. They view themselves as superior to the average person who possesses the same level of extraversion and openness. Since narcissists have such a high opinion of their abilities and intelligence, they feel more powerful than non-narcissists. Grandiose narcissism is a personality trait that maintains a person's self-esteem regardless of their surroundings. These individuals are independent of family, friends, and any other emotionally close relationships. They may appear to be a devoted spouse or a caring friend, but this is only for show. There is no genuine sincerity or devotion to their family members. The relationship is always centred on their own needs and desires. Their dependence on another is never motivated by emotions. Grandiose narcissists manifestly lack the necessary give and take for a normal, healthy relationship.

Personality Type and Leadership Positions

Due to their highly extroverted personality type, a grandiose type of narcissist may be ideally suited for leadership positions. They believe they are entitled to a position or promotion regardless of their inability to merit it. Extroverts with grandiose traits attempt to win the favor and goodwill of people who appear compliant and non-confrontational in order to feel more powerful and secure. If they do not receive praise and acknowledgement from others, they become hostile.

However, many grandiose narcissists succeed as organizational leaders and earn a great deal of money due to their charismatic appeal, audacity, and vision. Numerous studies suggest, for instance, that narcissistic CEOs were more receptive to making bold moves, such as betting on new technology, expanding their firms into international markets, and acquiring other businesses. However, research indicates that grandiose narcissists may put their companies' growth at risk for their own vested interests, which is not an ideal situation.

Since grandiose narcissists are typically impulsive, overconfident, and unwilling to heed expert advice, they frequently make poor choices. Because they're so full of themselves, they don't want to use objectivity before reaching a conclusion. They believe that if they select something, it must be of high quality. It is not incorrect for narcissists to be more intuitive than non-narcissists. However, even a hunch should be supported by logic and reason. Additionally, they do not value anyone's opinion because they constantly doubt others' knowledge, skills, and comprehension. Their superiority complex and overconfidence prevent them from interacting with others, understanding their perspectives, and being receptive to unconventional ideas. In order to have their way and satisfy their own egos, they will disregard data and research.

Chapter 3: Tipping Point

I yearned for a third child, but I knew it was not a good idea, especially given my recurrent illness. The stress of having a second child could become unbearable. As I reflected on my previous pregnancies, I realised that I had been completely alone in my expectant joy. Marty was never one of those husbands who gushed over his pregnant wife's beauty. I regret that I have only one photograph of myself during my pregnancy, in which I am not even in the centre. How could I have experienced two pregnancies without ever considering photographing the beauty of this miracle? Then I realised that my husband had never been impressed by its miraculous nature. I did not believe I was attractive because he did not. So why did we take a photograph?

I recalled the time when I first felt Aidan kick in my belly and asked Marty to place his hand on me so I could feel the baby move.

"That's just strange," he stated.

"Not at all! It's gorgeous! That is your child! I pleaded, "Kiss my stomach and let him know you're here and that you love him.

"Really?" he said with a shrug as I rubbed my stomach on the bed.

"Yes, in fact. I believe it is essential."

He said, "Whatever," as he knelt on the bed, leaned over, and kissed my stomach in the exact same spot where the baby had kicked. I laughed as Marty retreated, visibly annoyed and unimpressed by his first encounter with his son.

I knew that, regardless of how much I desired it, having another child with this man was utterly foolish.

I had another thought that I kept to myself and did not share with anyone: I might die and leave my children to be raised by their father. This thought terrified me to death. It seemed like the worst possible thing to do to these children I had worked so hard to bring into the world. My greatest fear was that I would not be able to protect them from having a childhood as dysfunctional as mine. My father did not handle the tragedy of my mother's passing in the best interest of my siblings and me, and I anticipated that Marty would be even worse.

I became increasingly aware of how egocentric my husband was, how his needs and desires always came first. I recalled how Marty would frown whenever he cleaned up after the children spilled something. Or he would tell them, "You're wasting my time," if he believed they were taking too long to do something on their own.

I suspected Aidan was afraid of Marty because he had begun to lie about things for fear of making his father angry. Marty frequently screamed at and lectured Aidan. Despite my repeated pleas for him to lighten up, he never did. I knew I had to protect my children from their father's passive-aggressive coping strategy. It would be selfish of me to add even more stress to my life by having another child, given that stress has the potential to take my life. The thought of my children going through life without the unconditional love I could give them was the driving force behind my decision that two children were sufficient.

I was constantly looking for inventive ways to earn more money. We purchased a rental property in 2005. It was twice the size recommended by the numerous books I had read on real estate investment, but Marty fell in love with the home and insisted on purchasing it. It turned into a nightmare, with delinquent tenants and home repairs we were unable to perform ourselves. I opened my own practise in 2006 with the hope of increasing my income, but when the recession hit, I was forced to work in other offices to pay the bills, which proved disastrous for my own practise. My attempts to improve our financial situation only served to make matters worse, while Marty appeared oblivious.

Marty discovered a mobile home on a permanent lot near Shawano Lake five years after we acquired the rental property and four years after I opened my practise (which was still not profitable). When he was a child, he lived there with his aunt. He was nostalgic for the numerous summers he spent at the lake as a child.

"This lake could provide my children with wonderful summer memories, as it did for me," he pleaded. He claimed to have these memories, but he had never shared them with me. Since he told me on our first date that he didn't learn how to swim until he was eighteen, I wondered how much fun he could have had at a lake during the summer.

The price of the mobile home was $10,000. Marty refused to accept no for an answer, and I once again found it so damn eerie that the price of this lot and trailer was identical to what I'd recently informed him was our home's approximate equity.

"Let's take the children there for a day to investigate. Marty stated, "It's the least you could do." "Then we can take the children to the beach for a pleasant day trip," he added.

"Okay, fine," I conceded, "but seriously, the rental is a money pit and my practise is still losing money. We will not purchase this!" I spoke with as much force as I could. Furthermore, maintaining this property in addition to our rental and primary residence would be a source of added stress.

When we arrived at the lake to view the mobile home, it was older, less attractive, and further from the water than I had been led to believe. Over the neighbor's fence, the lake was approximately one hundred yards away, and I could only see it if I stood on my tiptoes on the deck.

As we explored the interior of Marty's summer fantasy home, the owner stood and observed us.

No, this is not going to work out for us, I told the owner with a smile.

Marty gave me a hostile look.

The owner asked, "Are you certain? Why don't you take a moment to examine it again?"

"Thank you," Marty responded, "we will. Could you please wait by your truck so we can discuss it?"

"Sure," he replied as Marty led him to the mobile home's entrance. I was joking around with the children in an attempt to keep them preoccupied because I knew things were about to get ugly. There would be no physical contact, but the atmosphere would become extremely hostile, as it always did when Marty didn't get his way.

I decided to maintain my position this time. I sent the children outside to wait by the car, and I immediately began working before Marty could say anything. Simply put, we cannot afford it. And even if we were able to, I do not need the hassle of maintaining this shithole!"

"That's hogwash! You stated that there is money in the home. And this location is not that awful!"

"Goddamn it, Marty! Having equity in our home does not mean the money is hidden beneath a floorboard. It means we would have to go to a bank, get an appraisal on the house, and take out another loan, with associated fees, to completely deplete the minuscule amount of equity in that goddamn house! And after going through this process, we may discover that we don't have that much equity in the property to begin with. We cannot for the life of us do this!"

"So, what should I say to him now?" Marty grumbled.

"I don't give a f***! I said, "I'm not saying anything I haven't already said to you numerous times this week." "I'm here to enjoy a day at the beach with my children. Whatever you're doing here is your own goddamn business! I don't care what you tell him, I don't care if you tell him "we'll take it," but I can assure you that we will not."

I waited for Marty with our children at the car while he spoke with the owner. He returned to inform me that he had informed the man that he and I would discuss the matter and get back to him.

I said, "Whatever," while shaking my head.

We brought the children to the beach. The children and I enjoyed wading and floating in the waist-deep water, while Marty sulked next to us with his head hung low and remained silent. The children were nine and six years old. I knew they were picking up on the tension, especially Aidan, who I knew to be extremely sensitive, but they both played along with my attempts to ignore their father, who loomed over us like a massive, gloomy ogre.

He did not "win" the contest. I honestly do not know how I survived that day, but I did. I then realised that something had changed. I do not know whether the change occurred in me, him, or us, but it did not feel good. I knew I was doing the right thing, but I also sensed that I would eventually pay for it. This was the first time I had firmly refused Marty's request.

Chapter 4: They Never Offer An Apology Because They Believe They Are Always Right.

It is common to hear that people with NPD exhibit haughty attitudes and arrogant behaviours. Due to this, battling a narcissist may appear impossible.

According to Tawwab, there is no room for discussion or compromise with narcissists because they are always right. They will not always recognise an argument for what it is. They will simply perceive it as them imparting truth to you.

Weiler suggests avoiding negotiations and conflicts, despite the fact that the best course of action when dealing with someone with NPD is to end the relationship.

Lack of control and confrontation are what drives narcissists insane. She advises that the less control you give them by fighting back, the better.

Chapter 5: They Also Hardly Ever Apologize Because They Never Believe They Are Wrong.

They respond violently when you inform them that you are finished.

People with NPD frequently lash out at others when their self-esteem is damaged, making them extremely susceptible to humiliation and embarrassment.

According to Peykar, if you make it clear that you wish to end the relationship, the other party will intentionally harm you in retaliation.

"Their ego has been so severely injured that they become enraged and hostile toward everyone who has 'wronged' them. Given that everyone else is at fault, this is the case. "Except for the separation," she continues.

Narcissism

In 1898, British essayist and psychiatrist Havelock Ellis identified narcissism, also known as pathological self-absorption, as a mental disorder for the first time. Narcissism is characterised by a propensity to take others for granted or exploit them, an unusual coolness and composure that is only shaken when narcissistic confidence is threatened, and an exaggerated self-image and addiction to fantasy. The disorder is named after the mythological character Narcissus, who fell in love with his own reflection. According to Sigmund Freud, narcissism is a normal developmental stage in children, but it is considered a disorder after puberty.

Diagnosing narcissistic personality disorder typically involves clinical evaluation. In its fifth edition, the Diagnostic and Statistical Manual of Mental Disorders (DSM) describes it in terms of the personality traits grandiosity and attention-seeking, as well as significant impairments in personality functioning, such as excessively relying on others to regulate self-esteem, considering oneself exceptional, lacking empathy, and having predominantly superficial relationships (2013). These traits are unaffected by a medical condition, drug use, or a person's developmental stage, and they are relatively stable over time. Researchers have studied the narcissistic personality type, a less extreme form of narcissism. Despite exhibiting most or all of the symptoms of narcissistic personality disorder, it is believed that these individuals have a normal personality.

People with narcissistic personality disorder or the narcissistic personality type are preoccupied with maintaining overly positive self-perceptions. When they receive confirmation that others hold them in high regard or when they do not, they experience extreme positive or negative emotions, respectively, because they are overly concerned with receiving positive, flattering feedback from others. Because they desire positive feedback about themselves, narcissists actively manipulate others in order to solicit or coerce their admiration. Consequently, it is believed that narcissism is a manifestation of persistent interpersonal self-esteem regulation.

The narcissistic personality type is measured using self-report questionnaires such as the Narcissistic Personality Inventory (NPI), which is the most widely used scale and can also be used to evaluate narcissistic personality disorder. In the NPI, respondents are presented with a series of forced-choice questions in which they must decide which of two statements best describes them. People completing the NPI might be asked, for instance, which statement best describes them: "people always seem to recognise my authority" or "being an authority doesn't mean all that much to me." Individuals with high NPI scores have been shown to exhibit a variety of narcissistic traits, including arrogance, feigned superiority, and aggression. Moreover, those with a clinical diagnosis of narcissistic personality disorder have a higher NPI score than those in control groups or with other psychiatric diagnoses.

Clinical theories of narcissism, such as those of Austrian psychoanalysts Otto Kernberg and Heinz Kohut, assert that adult narcissism stems from childhood experiences. As the root cause of narcissistic personality disorder in adults, Kohut and Kernberg both point to early social (parental) relationships. In addition, both view narcissism as a fundamental flaw in healthy self-development. Kohut argues that the child's self-development and maturity are facilitated by interactions with other people, particularly the mother, who provides the child with opportunities to improve, gain approval, and identify with ideal and all-powerful role models. Two ways caring parents contribute to their children's self-development. First, they provide mirroring, which assists individuals in feeling more like themselves. Second, the limitations of parents cause their children to internalise or assume an attainable and realistic idealised image. Problems arise when a parent does not care about their child and does not provide them with approval or positive role models. According to Kohut, narcissism is essentially developmental arrest, a halt in the child's development at a normal and necessary stage, resulting in an inflated and unrealistic self-perception. Parallel to this, the child maintains an idealised view of others in order to maintain their sense of self-worth through social interaction.

On the other hand, according to Kernberg's theory, narcissism is a defence mechanism. It is the child's response to the parents' lack of warmth and empathy, which may be the result of their narcissism. Kernberg asserts that the child becomes emotionally malnourished and enraged as a result of parental neglect. According to this perspective, the child's narcissistic defence ultimately results in an inflated and grandiose sense of self. This defence reflects the child's attempt to hide in an admirable aspect of himself. Kernberg believes that narcissists are ostentatious on the outside but insecure and self-doubting on the inside.

Adult narcissists, according to both the theories of Kernberg and Kohut, have a grandiose view of the self and a conflicted psychological dependence on others. They also have a history of unsatisfactory childhood social relationships.

Does a tree make a sound when it falls in the forest when no one is around to hear it? Is it truly a success if no one is present to witness a narcissist's achievement? In this case, the answer is negative. If they were not commended and acknowledged, they might as well have made no progress at all. Because they only derive satisfaction from the admiration of others, the victory is rendered meaningless.

They behave as if they are flawless. They excel at everything more than anyone else. All of their possessions are superior to yours. There is no way that they could be imperfect in any way, so if someone claims that they have a flaw, it must be a mistake.

Never content with who they are and what they have, they are never satisfied. They frequently fantasise about a better life, profession, or appearance. They find nothing about their lives to be truly satisfying. Even though they believe they deserve better, they make no effort to accomplish their goals.

They cannot handle witnessing the success of others. They will find a way to undermine their success in order to maintain their dominance, as they are incapable of containing their envy. The adage "misery loves company" rings all too true in this situation.

They may appear concerned, but they are indifferent to the troubles of others. They gain from this. This eliminates one person who is doing well in the world, thereby making them feel better about themselves.

They do not recognise the value of others. They only view others as valuable when they can benefit from them. Narcissists socialise frequently with other narcissists. The "outstanding" individuals. "The Elite"No one else merits their attention.

Narcissists must always, or at least appear to, be performing better than their peers. They thrive on being manipulative and in control. If they do not feel in complete control, they will not be truly happy. They demand recognition for their efforts and worship for themselves and others. Typically, narcissists gravitate toward occupations and hobbies that put them in the spotlight.

Typically, narcissistic traits begin to manifest in early adulthood. predominantly in men 50 to 70 percent of individuals with Narcissistic Personality Disorder are male. This has no identified cause. It may be due to a combination of childhood experiences, upbringing, and chemical makeup.

Throughout their lives, boys are typically taught that they are superior and unique. Although this may appear to be positive reinforcement, these boys may develop a sense of superiority over others as a result of receiving inappropriate praise.

Narcissism is a highly toxic behaviour that will repel anyone who recognises these problematic traits from your life. As a result, individuals with this disorder typically have few friends and spend the majority of their time alone. They mistake other people's rejection for their own. Since they are superior to everyone else and nobody is deserving of their time.

Chapter 6: Narcissistic Abuse Cycle

The narcissistic abuse cycle is a pattern of abusive behaviour that characterises the relationships of narcissists. It involves idealising a person, devaluing them, repeating the cycle, and then discarding them when they are no longer useful.

Although narcissistic traits are widespread, the intensity of these characteristics varies. It should be noted that a person may be involved in a narcissistic abuse cycle with a person who does not meet all of the criteria for NPD but displays NPD symptoms.

This article explores the various stages of the narcissistic abuse cycle, the mental health repercussions of narcissistic abuse, and some potentially helpful coping mechanisms.

Cycle of Narcissistic Abuse Phases

Listed below are characteristics of the narcissistic abuse cycle.

This phase, also known as the appreciation phase, is characterised by love bombing.

Instantaneously, the narcissist connects with you. They exalt you and place you on a pedestal, making you feel unique and beautiful. Regardless of the nature of the relationship (romantic, platonic, professional, etc.), it moves quickly and has a fiery quality.

In a romantic relationship, the narcissist will be lavish with gifts and compliments. They will make you feel unique and appear infatuated with you. It will appear as if they have fallen instantly in love with you, and it will feel inevitable.

Even if they appear innocent or even endearing, there may be early indications of controlling strategies. For instance, they may shame you for spending time with people outside of the relationship or for exceeding previously established boundaries.

In a friendship, the narcissist lavishes you with praise, spends a great deal of time with you, and relies on you for everything.

When you work for a narcissistic boss, you'll have the impression that you're their ideal employee and that no one else is as skilled as you. There will be hints of raises and promotions that never materialise.

Chapter 7: What To Do In Response To Signs Of Emotional Manipulation

One of the most essential aspects of manipulation is gaslighting, a conversational technique designed to disconnect you from your gut instincts or rational assessments of the world.

If you find yourself questioning your sincerity or "sanity," this is a sign that something is amiss and manipulation may be occurring.

When you question your reality, it is easier for a manipulator to persuade and convince you to conform to their vision. The primary goal of gaslighting is to detach someone from their reality and sow doubt in their mind or the minds of others so that the person who is gaslighting can get away with anything or maintain the perception of control over others.

The relationship is very emotionally intense.

Manipulation in romantic relationships typically entails establishing an emotional and passionate bond that serves as the basis for attempting to maintain control.

Love bombing, turmoil, and intensity are common and necessary characteristics for manipulative effectiveness. A common tactic employed by manipulative and abusive partners is to keep their romantic partners confused, perplexed, and preoccupied with fantasies of what is to come or the wonderful moments that have occurred.

You Fear Being Abandoned.

If someone is being manipulated, they may experience uncertainty, anxiety, or confusion.

Many victims may mistake the signs of manipulation for the normal give-and-take in a relationship. However, you can distinguish between healthy compromise and harmful manipulation based on the presence or absence of fear. With compromise, the thought "If I don't do what that person says, they will leave or hurt me" will be eliminated.

If this concern enters your mind or you feel it in your stomach, you are likely being exploited.

You have an intuition that something is amiss.

Listening to your intuition is essential for detecting deception. The enteric nervous system, which is a component of the Autonomic Nervous System, resides in the intestines and gut and is responsible for detecting sensory inputs and transmitting them to the brain. Their combined efforts are intended to assess danger, and this often occurs without our conscious awareness, which we interpret as a "gut feeling."

You Feel Insecure.

The goal of manipulation is to maintain control over you, and making you feel terrible about yourself may be one way manipulators maintain their authority and keep you complacent. They take advantage of your vulnerability. When you are weak, they use your fears and vulnerabilities against you in order to feel superior.

They want you to depend solely on them.

If you have no other options, it is easier for the manipulator to exert control over you. Therefore, attempts at isolation or severe codependence may be indicative of manipulation. They attempt to isolate you (physically, socially, and financially) and cultivate your reliance on them. When you limit your resources and external influences, you give them control.

They Compare You Constantly to Others.

Manipulative personalities thrive on the belief that others will vie for their position. Constant comparison to others may be a form of manipulation because it is intended to evoke feelings of inferiority and competition.

They've managed to gain the support of your friends and family.

We must keep an eye out for more than just undesirable characteristics. Be on the lookout for ingratiating actions or other efforts to be perceived in a positive light, as this is typically a deliberate attempt to increase the distance between the victim and their support system by fostering the perception of uncertainty.

Manipulators may contact family members or close friends without informing their partners. If it were a kind gesture, it would result in more enjoyable excursions or an expanded social circle for both partners. Instead, it is manipulation when such conversations create a smokescreen, exacerbate internal conflict, or increase isolation. In such situations, the victim's family and friends may become unwitting participants in a psychological game the manipulator is trying to win.

Chapter 8: Tips For Surviving The Breakup

You ended your relationship with the narcissist. What now? You are likely emotionally drained after ending a relationship with someone who constantly demeans, criticises, and gaslights you. Narcissists will never experience satisfaction in any aspect of their lives, including relationships, because nothing is ever unique enough for them.

Depending on the state of mind your narcissist partner is in when you announce your intention to end the relationship, leaving a narcissist may be difficult or slightly less difficult. If they are in a mentally depleted state, you will likely encounter either passive aggression or overt anger. Alternatively, if they are in a good mood, the narcissist may attempt to "love bomb" you in an attempt to win you back and convince you to stay. In any case, the best course of action is to be prepared for any eventuality.

Despite the fact that breaking up with a narcissist will never be easy, there are steps you can take after the breakup to ensure the best possible outcome. Here are eight survival tips for ending a relationship with a narcissist.

Remove all traces of your past relationship.

Because a narcissist needs to create the impression that you are special, or to feel special themselves, he or she has likely given you extravagant gifts or taken you on extravagant trips to give you the impression that you have a wonderful life together. However, these items can make it difficult to recall the difficult times and your reasons for wanting to end the relationship. Remove all gifts and photographs that remind you of your partner from your home. If you insist on keeping them, place them in a box and store them in the attic. However, if you see reminders of the good times, you could easily convince yourself that things weren't as bad as you believed they were prior to the breakup. The best recommendation would be to eradicate all memories of the narcissist permanently.

Do not grant them "one last chance."

Before finally leaving an abusive relationship, the average person tries seven times. It is impossible to predict whether they will be physically violent with you, especially if they have been violent in the past. You should never give them another opportunity to emotionally or physically harm you. Once you have had enough, you must give up forever. No additional "second chances"

Learn how to become grounded.

Because you may still be reliving the experience in your mind, it is crucial to regain your composure after an abusive relationship, which is frequently traumatic. The majority of individuals who end an abusive narcissistic relationship will literally relive everything. Even though you are no longer physically experiencing it, the tastes, smells, and other sensations will often still feel very real to you. It is similar to post-traumatic stress disorder, and unless you work through it, it will feel as though it will consume your entire life. You must determine why you were initially attracted to the narcissist and ensure that you do not fall for the same type of person again. You must completely reclaim your body and mind.

4. Avoid rushing into a new relationship.

Due to what is known as repetition compulsion, many individuals repeatedly date similar individuals. Essentially, you are attempting to mend a past trauma with the present. After experiencing abuse, you may even seek out abusive individuals in an attempt to change or reform them. Or you may end up with people who mistreat you and manipulate or control you simply because the situation feels familiar. Prior to entering another relationship, it is crucial that you work through your pain so that you do not continue to be hurt. After you have healed and realised what you truly want and need in a partner, you will be ready to find someone who truly deserves you. Then and only then will you be prepared for a new relationship.

5. Keep yourself busy.

It is equally important to stay busy after a breakup with a narcissist as it is to allow yourself to experience loss and grief. Consider activities you can engage in when you require a distraction. Learn more about your interests, engage in physical activity, or even start a new hobby. It is time to focus on yourself, as your needs were likely neglected throughout this relationship. It is time to pursue your passions and true happiness.

Surround yourself with supportive and positive individuals.

A narcissist will attempt to isolate you from your social support network. They will require such a high level of commitment and loyalty that you may lose touch with friends and family over the course of the relationship. You should attempt to reconnect with those who truly know and care about you and inform them of your current predicament and support requirements. During the initial few weeks of your transition, you may wish to have your support network check in with you daily.

Consider blocking any mutual friends you and your partner may share.

Make sure to inform your friends that you do not want to hear about the narcissist's life or why you made a mistake by leaving him. Because your mental health depends on avoiding the narcissist as much as possible, it may be necessary to block these mutual friends. Mutual friends will likely attempt to persuade you to rejoin them or continue sending you updates. In order to convince you to return to the relationship, a narcissist may ask a mutual friend to speak to you on their behalf and try to convince you otherwise. It is highly likely that the narcissist treats these "friends" differently than he treats you; therefore, they cannot know the narcissist in the same way that you do. They simply lack comprehension.

Chapter 9: Adaptive Strategies To Help You Avoid

The narcissist will likely not leave you alone after you leave the room. They will do everything possible to remain a part of your life in some capacity. When a partner attempts to end a relationship with a narcissist, the narcissist will perceive it as a supply cutoff rather than a loss of companionship. The narcissist must continue to meet his supply needs.

A narcissist will attempt to reestablish contact because they are unable to function without affection and attention, not because they love or care about you. You will suffer greatly after leaving a narcissistic relationship if you are unable to recognise the mental manipulation for what it is.

A narcissist will do anything they can to make you doubt not only yourself, but also the circumstances surrounding your broken relationship. They will spin their own versions of past events in an attempt to convince you to return. You must maintain a firm grasp on reality and mental fortitude at all times so that their lies do not misrepresent what actually transpired during your relationship and time together.

In this chapter, we will discuss several coping mechanisms that will assist you in resisting the narcissist's attempts to win you back. You should be able to comprehend why they are saying these hurtful things and not let them have the intended effect on you.

Having a narcissistic partner can cause you to develop limiting beliefs about yourself, the relationship, and the narcissist. Some examples of such beliefs include:

You must recognise, however, that none of these beliefs are true. Your love will never triumph over their inability to love. You can find more fulfilment elsewhere. Because they have not seen the error of their ways, it is impossible to return to the previous state of affairs. You are in no way responsible for the breakup of the relationship. You are not responsible for fixing them, nor could you if you tried. They absolutely do not share your sentiments. Literally, none of these beliefs are true in the slightest.

You must be kind to yourself as you end the relationship with a narcissist. You must recognise that you deserve significantly more. All you have to do is call upon your latent inner strength, which has always been in the background.

It will take you longer to recover from a narcissistic relationship than a healthy one. You must exercise self-patience. Recognize that difficult times lie ahead, but you can and will prevail to tell your tale. You should practise self-kindness every day because the more you do it, the more it becomes ingrained in your heart until it becomes more natural each day.

Because it took the narcissist considerable time to wear you down and shape you to their liking, it will take you roughly the same amount of time to return to your original self. Remember to take things one day at a time and to have the patience you need to recover, regardless of how long it takes. Recovery will depend on the severity and depth of your pain as well as the duration of your suffering.

Relearning what it means to be you will play a significant role in your healing process. To avoid similar relationships in the future, you must reassemble the fragments of your true self, even if you need the assistance of loved ones or a professional therapist.

You will prevail over the narcissist if you can gain a little strength every day. Maintaining an upward trajectory, despite setbacks, is the only sure way to rediscover one's true self. Never again allow your power and dignity to be diminished. In fact, your narcissistic partner and your relationship together should have taught you a valuable lesson and improved your ability to identify narcissists in the future. Thus, narcissistic relationships can be avoided at all costs.

This book's contents are an excellent resource for self-education, since knowledge is the source of power. You will be better able to anticipate a narcissist's next move once you have a firm grasp of what you are up against. When narcissists are discovered, they lose their competitive edge. You will have the upper hand if you are better prepared.

The fewer interactions with a narcissist you have, the better off you will be. Because a narcissist will always be toxic, you can recover and heal much quicker with minimal contact. They are incapable of change. Co-parenting is extremely challenging for narcissists, so exercise caution if you have children with an ex-spouse. Find a family member or mediator who can act as a buffer between you and the narcissist, as the narcissist is likely to behave better in the presence of others, which can reduce your anxiety. The less contact you have with the narcissist, the better it will be for your children, who do not need to see you fighting.

The process of separating from a toxic, narcissistic ex-partner can be very stressful. As a coping mechanism, numerous victims of narcissistic abuse deny the emotional and domestic abuse. Many suffer from extreme anxiety, low self-esteem, and Post-Traumatic Stress Disorder (PTSD). Because the brain secretes chemicals when in this heightened fight-or-flight state, this type of abuse is frequently addictive, which is what causes the victim to permit the abuse to continue.

When you begin to heal yourself, develop coping mechanisms, and develop self-confidence, the narcissist's power will diminish. You will no longer be susceptible to mental and emotional manipulation. In fact, you will flourish in the future because narcissists lose interest when their manipulative behaviours no longer work.

Chapter 10: Do Individuals With Narcissism Enjoy Kissing?

The notion that narcissists dislike kissing stems from their inability to recognise and identify with the needs of others. Sex, kissing, and cuddling can satisfy essential physical needs, but they can also foster bonding and deepen intimacy. A person who does not feel the need to bond may not have much time for nonsexual affection such as kissing or cuddling because they believe, "This doesn't benefit me much, so why bother?"

In the early stages of the relationship, they may pay close attention to your requirements. Later, sex may appear routine or give you the impression that they only care about their own desires. On the other hand, they may be pretending to be someone they are not to gain your admiration. They may require your approval to be effective, and you may perceive that they are using your admiration to advance their career. If you share their interests and have nothing but positive things to say about their work, you will most likely encounter no difficulties. However, it may be difficult to form strong bonds with them. If they do not feel the need to invest in a deeper relationship, physical affection may lack the intimacy you seek. If you want to spend more time kissing and cuddling, but your partner does not, you may be disappointed. Unless they view kissing as a means of demonstrating their prowess and gaining your admiration. If they perceive it as a means to obtain something they desire, they may be more willing to participate. Relationships can often be improved through therapy, provided both parties are willing to make an effort to alter.

Chapter 11: Disordered Narcissism

When Narcissists Develop Pathology

Collins English Dictionary states, "You label a person or their behaviour as pathological when they behave in an excessive and undesirable manner and have extreme, uncontrollable emotions." Having to do with pathology or illness is their second definition. Both definitions are applicable to this article. Lastly, pathology is the behaviour of a disease or condition, which enables an accurate diagnosis.

After defining our terms precisely, let's investigate what happens when narcissism crosses the threshold into disease.

A person is not deemed pathologically narcissistic before receiving an official diagnosis from a psychologist.

When narcissism becomes pathological, certain characteristics will stand out to you. You will suddenly comprehend why people behave in particular ways. The following are the most noteworthy items:

They may have a large social circle, but few or no close friends. They fear that a close relationship would require them to reveal all their secrets.

If you are married to a narcissist, you will notice that connection is restricted. Little to no emotional connection exists. It has the air of a business transaction.

Even the smallest criticism will enrage them. In reality, they cannot be viewed as imperfect and prevent you from appropriately emphasising anything.

They are convinced that they are right and that everyone else is wrong.

By isolating everyone, they are able to continually advance their desire to dominate others. Everyone is permitted to lie to maintain their false identity so long as they are kept apart.

They will soon abandon you if you fail to satisfy their demand for continuous praise.

If they believe someone could provide them with narcissistic supply, they will "love bomb" that individual. This transcends mere love bombing. If it means receiving reciprocal adoration, they will treat even distant acquaintances as if they are the greatest person in the world.

In addition, all of these external opinions must always be positive. This is where you come in; you have been hired to soothe their extremely fragile ego.

They require only someone who will love, obey, and serve them, and not someone who will love them.

When they possess it, they will be in the ideal position. Similar to hiring an employee to perform a particular service.

Please yourself by reading the fine print. There you will see that they will have the right to blame, insult, and devalue you at certain points. To feel better about themselves, or alternatively to discipline you back into submission, and you must consent to this whenever they deem it necessary.

You are required to eliminate the word "I" from your vocabulary and replace it with "We and you."

However, your employer will retain "I" on all levels.

Additionally, you are not permitted to have an opinion or think independently. It is highly recommended to express total agreement with all of their statements.

When they require your assistance, you should run and not walk.

If you are uncertain about anything, you should seek resolution from them. Do not communicate with anyone else.

You agree, by entering into this contract, that they will be the most important person in your life and that you will always put their desires before your own or your own best interests.

You are expected to abandon your family and friends in favour of adopting theirs. It is however preferred that you have no friends whatsoever.

If and when you decide to leave without their express permission and of your own volition, you will face severe punishment. These are the fundamental rules.

Consequently, everything revolves around them and not you.

You are merely occupying space and performing a function that could be performed by any willing individual. You are there to acknowledge their existence, uphold all of their opinions, tell everyone, including them, how wonderful they are, and express pity for their plight when necessary.

Chapter 12: Can A Narcissistic Change?

If you've ever conducted research to determine whether someone you know is a narcissist, you've likely come across numerous articles claiming that narcissists are inherently evil and unchangeable.

However, these assumptions do not reflect the complexities of narcissism. Everyone has the ability to change, in reality. Many individuals with narcissism simply lack motivation or face other obstacles.

How can you determine if a person is willing to change?

Some individuals with narcissistic tendencies may be resistant to change.

However, others do. How can you tell if you or a loved one is prepared for a change? There is no single correct response.

The following indicators suggest that a person is willing to examine their behaviour and try out new methods of change.

Understanding the feelings of others

Many individuals confuse "narcissism" with "lack of empathy." While people with narcissistic tendencies frequently find it difficult to consider the feelings and perspectives of others, research from 2014 indicates that empathy is not always absent, despite the fact that it is frequently lacking. When motivated, people with narcissism can develop greater empathy, particularly when considering the experiences of their children or others who admire or value them.

A person who expresses affection or concern for particular individuals may be prepared for further change in therapy.

Concern for their actions

A person who is interested in understanding why they behave as they do may be willing to explore their behaviour in therapy. This interest may be sparked by reading articles or books about narcissism, or by someone pointing out their narcissistic tendencies. People with narcissistic characteristics can function adequately in daily life. Intelligence and ambition can pique a person's interest not only in his or her own behaviour, but also in that of others. This can result in a shift toward viewing others as equals rather than inferiors.

Willingness to consider oneself

Self-reflection can be challenging for narcissists due to the erosion of their protective shell of perfection. A key trait of narcissism is the inability to see the positive and negative characteristics that all people possess (known as whole object relations).

Instead, the majority of narcissists view people, including themselves, as either completely good (perfect) or completely bad (worthless). If their belief in their own perfection is questioned, they may lash out or fall into a cycle of shame and self-hatred. Those who are capable of examining and reflecting on negative behaviours without devaluing the critic or themselves may be prepared for a deeper dive.

Dual diagnosis

People with narcissistic tendencies frequently suffer from depression, anxiety, anorexia nervosa, and substance abuse. People typically seek therapy for reasons other than narcissistic characteristics. The desire to alleviate current emotional pain and avoid future suffering may be a potent impetus for change-seeking behaviour.

How does the treatment appear?

A therapist who has received specialised training in dealing with narcissism and narcissistic personality disorder is best suited to address narcissistic issues (NPD).

There are numerous methods for addressing narcissism, but therapy typically involves the following steps:

- recognising existing defence mechanisms
- investigating the reasons for these coping mechanisms
- learning and practising new behavioral patterns
- investigating how one's actions affect others
- examining the connections between their internal voice and how they treat others

Frequently, the key to long-term progress lies in:

- assisting them in exploring the causes of their narcissistic defences without judgement or criticism
- providing confirmation
- promoting self-forgiveness and self-compassion in order to cope with shame and vulnerability

Finding the appropriate type of therapy

There are a few therapies that are particularly effective in treating narcissism.

Schema therapy, a relatively new treatment approach that has been demonstrated to be effective in the treatment of narcissism, assists individuals in addressing trauma from early experiences that may have contributed to narcissistic defences.

- Another beneficial therapy is Gestalt therapy.

- CBT
- transference-centered psychotherapy
- psychoanalysis

Dr. Wheeler also stresses the significance of group therapy for individuals with personality disorders. Group therapy enables individuals to perceive how others view them. Additionally, it enables individuals to observe how various aspects of their personalities affect others.

How to Provide Assistance During Treatment

Although the origins of personality disorders are unknown, narcissistic tendencies typically develop as a form of self-defense. In other words, many narcissists were raised by narcissistic parents or were abused or neglected as children. They internalise the criticism and negative messages they receive.

They develop maladaptive coping strategies, also known as narcissistic defences, to combat this negative voice. Typically, their behaviour toward others reflects how they perceive themselves. If someone you care about has decided to seek treatment for narcissism, you can assist them in the following ways:

Provide words of affirmation and encouragement

People with narcissism typically respond positively to compliments. They may want to demonstrate their abilities by performing well, especially as therapy begins. Your acknowledgement of their efforts may encourage them to persist, thereby increasing the likelihood that the therapy will be successful.

Recognize when progress is being made.

Therapy for narcissism can be time-intensive, and progress may be gradual. You may notice changes early on, such as attempts to control outbursts and avoid dishonesty or manipulation. Nevertheless, certain behaviours, such as anger in response to perceived criticism, may persist.

Working with your own therapist can help you learn to recognise improvements and determine what behavioral changes are necessary to maintain the relationship.

Determine the characteristics of behaviours involving apologies.

Therapy may involve recognising problematic behaviour and learning to make amends. However, the individual will likely continue to struggle with admitting wrongdoing and offering sincere apologies. Instead of discussing the situation or saying "I'm sorry," they may offer you a nice dinner or do something nice.

Chapter 13: The Overt Narcissist

The overt narcissist is loud, in stark contrast to the covert narcissist. The overt narcissist, also known as a grandiose narcissist, is deeply convinced that he is superior to everyone else. He employs his superiority complex to motivate himself to pursue power above all else. He desires positions of authority or management and will trample others to attain them.

He is unconcerned with the thoughts of others, including their perceptions of himself. According to him, those who look down on him are too stupid or incompetent to recognise his worth, and he rejects their ideas entirely. Their inability to recognise greatness when it stares them in the face renders them disrespectful in the eyes of the narcissist.

The manifest narcissist is boisterous and unafraid to assert his sense of superiority. He may sit in restaurants and speak condescendingly to the waiter, believing that the waiter should have attended school if he wished to be regarded as respectable. As that is the cashier's job, he may place the money he is using to pay for groceries on the counter for her to collect; he should not do her job for her. He may even declare aloud that the grocery store bagger must be an idiot if he cannot separate his bread and oranges so that the bread is not crushed. When the bagger dares to comment, the narcissist will throw any evidence of his superiority in his direction.

This type of narcissist is typically much more obnoxious to be around than covert narcissists, and you immediately recognise his presence when he enters the room. The narcissist will let you know through his actions and words that he is a narcissist, just as the joke goes that you can tell when someone is a vegan by what they say.

The overt narcissist typically develops this type of personality either as a coping mechanism, like the covert narcissist, or as a result of being repeatedly told as a child that he is superior to others for whatever reason. He may have been born into a wealthy family and had domestic servants around him from an early age, or he may have internalised that his effortless school performance, in which he consistently outperformed everyone in his class with no effort, meant he was superior in every way. He opts to demonstrate this elsewhere. Regardless of the cause, the result is someone who is arrogant and believes he is superior to everyone else, despite the fact that we all bleed the same, eat the same, and sleep the same. He does not respect others because he believes he is superior, and he displays this attitude frequently.

The blatant narcissist can frequently boast about his recent successes and accomplishments without being coaxed to do so. He will brag about his recent accomplishments, sometimes embellishing his participation in events or projects to make himself look better. The only time he cares about another person's opinion of him is when it is positive; anything negative will be disregarded.

This extends to the narcissist's interpersonal relationships. He does not care what his partner thinks of him and will not bother trying to make her fall in love with him after the initial love-bombing phase to hook her. However, the narcissist is concerned with whether he can continue to use her as a tool. As far as he is concerned, his romantic partners only serve as instruments. They are only useful when obedient; if they deviate from his expectations, he will discard them and move on to someone else.

Under no circumstances will the blatant narcissist apologise to someone he perceives as inferior to him. He may consider apologising to a peer or superior, but it's a remote possibility. He has no intention of stooping to the level of a commoner in order to apologise, as he does not see the point in doing so. At best, he will be forced to offer a cursory "I'm sorry you feel that way" if he is pushed into a corner. This, however, is a non-apology that does nothing more than shift the blame onto the other party. Ultimately, the narcissist does not control the emotions of others.

www.ingramcontent.com/pod-product-compliance
Lightning Source LLC
Chambersburg PA
CBHW070309120526
44590CB00017B/2601